WOUNDED WARRIORS of TIME

H. Oral Brown

authorHOUSE®

AuthorHouse™
1663 Liberty Drive
Bloomington, IN 47403
www.authorhouse.com
Phone: 1 (800) 839-8640

Published by AuthorHouse: 07/08/2015

ISBN: 978-1-5049-1290-7 (sc)
ISBN: 978-1-5049-1289-1 (e)

Scripture quotations marked KJV are from the Holy Bible, King James
Version (Authorized Version). First published in 1611. Quoted from the KJV
Classic Reference Bible, Copyright © 1983 by The Zondervan Corporation.

Scripture quotations marked "NCV" are taken from the New Century
Version, Copyright © 1987, 1988, 1991 by Word Publishing, a division
of Thomas Nelson, Inc. Used by permission. All rights reserved.

Scripture quotations marked NASB are taken from the New American
Standard Bible®, Copyright © 1960, 1962, 1963, 1968, 1971, 1972, 1973,
1975, 1977, 1995 by The Lockman Foundation. Used by permission.

Print information available on the last page.

Any people depicted in stock imagery provided by Thinkstock are models,
and such images are being used for illustrative purposes only.
Certain stock imagery © Thinkstock.

This book is printed on acid-free paper.

FOREWORD

**"Biblically, waiting is not just something
we have to do until we get what we want.
Waiting is part of the process of becoming
what God wants us to be. – John Ortberg**

As much as it may appear to be an accident or mishap, nothing happens before it's time. Timing is everything. We live in time, by time and for time. God on the other hand, does not live in the capsule of time nor is He controlled by time. Yet, He uses the process of time to accomplish His divine purpose in our lives.

The scriptures confirm the fact that while God is not controlled by time, He waits for the fullness of time (Galatians 4:4-5) or the set time (Psalm 102:13) even as He works through the process of shaping and molding us in the meantime.

I agree with H. Oral Brown that far too often, we find ourselves being defeated in the "waiting" battle. Many believers are failing and falling short of the manifested presence and power of God because they are not willing to wait for the fullness of time. It is imperative that we understand that the promise is wrapped up in the process. Since we live within the boundaries of time, it is vital that we understand that if we don't have the will to wait, we will become wounded by time.

In "Wounded Warriors of Time," H. Oral Brown shares some of his life's experiences and response to waiting. Some of his responses, as he indicates were not always the right response. As he revealed in this book, ultimately he had to pay the price for not waiting. I am deeply moved by his humility as a Pastor in sharing some of his shortcomings as he waits for God.

How should believers respond to the waiting process? What should be our attitude while we are waiting? What are the rewards for waiting? In this book, Brown reveals the answer to these and other pertinent questions.

It is my prayer that the message in this book permeates and ultimately transform your entire life as you wait for the full manifestation of the promises of God in your life. "We are all warriors of time through having to wait on, and wrestle within its borders." It is my prayer that you apply the message in this book so that no matter what you face in life, you will be equipped to overcome, because you have been anointed to "Walk in Victory."

His Grace, Bishop Neil C. Ellis CMG, DD, DHL, PHD
Presiding Bishop Global United Fellowship
Senior Pastor/Teacher Mount Tabor Church
Nassau, Bahamas

ACKNOWLEDGEMENT

It is with profound gratitude that I pause to pay tribute to persons who have assisted in the production of this book entitled 'Wounded Warriors of Time." Needless to say that at the beginning of this document my physical position was better than it is today, but will change with God's will.

The pressure of writing a book is by no means a small challenge as its demands ones time, resources and energy in order to produce an acceptable manuscript. Because of what I personally experienced physically at the end of writing this book it was humanely impossible to complete it without a sense of physical accomplishment, it required help from persons whose hearts have been touched by God to be able to rise to the challenge of doing a lot of footwork and manuscript writing.

I acknowledge with thanks Elder Rochelle Johnson, Pastor France George and my wife Mrs. Marion Brown who took up the challenge to see this effort to its conclusion. Let it not be thought that these few words express my total appreciation to them in any small way, let it be seen as words of sincerity from the heart of a grateful author.

Finally I acknowledge with appreciation words of commendation from His Grace Bishop Neil C Ellis who personally encouraged me to write this book and to forward it with words encouraging persons to read and to be spiritually uplifted.

May God bless them always and in all ways.

PREFACE

There is no one alive or dead, who can lay claim to not having to go through a period of waiting. If it's not on a doctor's visit, a bus arrival, Christmas celebration or even for a good meal to be completed, there exists that element of time in waiting.

Far too often, we find ourselves defeated in the battle of having to wait. When this happens, much is lost and we become like one who is a wounded warrior.

This book steps beyond the traditional thought pattern of how we react when waiting on every day events, and goes into the area of waiting in the spiritual realm. For example, how we react when having to wait on a particular concert to begin; to having to wait on a prayer request, or a mighty move of God in situations needing His intervention.

In as much as we know that the God we serve supersedes time, and is not controlled by seconds, hours, days or years, we still try to place Him within the realms of time.

We expect things that we request from Him, to happen within a given period. When this is not to be, we as God's children become worried and begin to take things into our own hands. Many are the scenes of defeat and disaster, along our struggling path, because we chose to take matters into our own hands.

I have witnessed families struggling through a financial crisis, and even though they would have prayed fervently, nothing seemed to change. Then finally after a time, they decided to give up on God. They stopped sowing seed, tithing and trusting in Him. To them, the wait was unbearable. The sad thing about it all was that I, as pastor, was unable to help them. My inability, then, to advise them intelligently on what they should be doing while waiting on God, did more harm than good to a volatile situation.

It is while looking at all of the wounded saints of the past that I have been inspired to write this book.

I wish all who read it, to properly investigate what it means to wait on God, through applying His standard in waiting. Get to really know who is the creator of time, but functions out of its realm.

Yes, many who have tried to explain the very existence of God as being beyond time, agree with me, and describe Him as Ontological. His existence they would say, was as from the beginning, even before time began. However we still end up placing a time limit on Him.

So, it has been my sincere wish that this book will help you as Christians to really see who and not what you assume to be waiting on. He is a timeless God, and that is truly who He is. We must therefore be careful of the waiting signs that we give off, which may speak to the opposite of what we believe. In that regard, I have dedicated one of the chapters of this book, to the topic "Waiting Signs."

Many other topics will be discussed, such as, "The weightiness in Waiting," and "Time makes or breaks Faith."

Brothers and Sisters, I reiterate, there is no argument against the statement that we are all warriors of time through having to wait on and wrestle within its borders. But we have not always been very successful in the combat. Some of us have been mortally wounded, and often times, beyond repair.

Let us make up in our mind to improve the fighting techniques that are necessary for us to be victorious warriors with time, knowing how to wait successfully.

It is my honest prayer that as I was led by the Holy Spirit to write this book, it will help us in our waiting so to do.

Brothers and sisters, we are all time warriors, who have been destined to win.

INTRODUCTION

In June 3, 1993, The Lord called me to pastor one of the units in His great army of Witnesses. I was granted the awesome privilege to give the unit a name. It was called Heritage Missionary Baptist Church.

Although I had been working administratively in other churches, pastoring would be to me, a brand new field of endeavor, hence I would have to, at the age of fifty, begin to function in a new way, embracing a new paradigm shift.

My responsibility would no longer be that of following while others lead, but to lead while others follow. It was not for me to carry out instructions handed to me, but rather, mine to command.

In my position as Pastor, I was advised that there were four major functions that have characterized the way pastoral care has been practiced in the history of the Christian ministry. These four functions are, healing, sustaining, guiding and reconciling:

Healing consisted of binding up the wounds, repairing damage that has been done as a result of disease, infection, or invasion; restoring a condition that has been lost.

Sustaining refers to helping persons courageously and creatively endure and transcend difficult situations while preventing or lessening the impact of the situation; sustaining is offered when healing is not possible.

Guiding seeks to help persons in trouble make confident choices between alternative courses of action that will help them solve the problem they are facing.

Reconciliation seeks to reestablish broken relationships between a person and God on the one hand; and between a person and other persons on the other.

In addition, there were many other responsibilities for which the pastor was also equally responsible, and which carried with them just as much importance as those four points mentioned.

So again at the senior age of fifty, it was incumbent upon me to hit the ground running, with innovative programs, exciting activities, spiritually motivated ideas and a building programme comparable to the present time, and complimenting those previously mentioned.

In my mind's eye, this meant that there would be no time for dragging of the feet. Simply put, I would need all hands on deck, excited and supportive. I would need a strong financial backing to move successfully forward. I would need a strong group of saints whose heart God has truly touched, and were inspired to run in this race. The task before us was enormous. It's goals were lofty. It's vision clear. In fact, the Mission Statement for Heritage Missionary Baptist church states : (and I quote)

"Empowered to share the full Gospel of Jesus Christ with those we are privileged to meet, and to see lives transformed spiritually, socially, and educationally, for the building of the Kingdom and to the Glory of God."

Sitting still idly by and waiting on a God who would take His time to answer me when I pray, would pose a major problem. I did not have time to wait, I was fifty years old. I had a briefcase of plans to bring to fruition, and a whole lot of people who were anxious for us to succeed, and yet countless others who wanted us to fail. I did not have the time to wait on God. I believed in praying to Him, but not waiting on Him. Time was of the essence. I convinced myself that whatever good thing I prayed for, that was cleared automatically. I consoled myself that His word declared that no good thing will He withhold from them that walked upright. That's where I got myself into trouble.

There were times as a Christian I did not walk upright, but I felt prepared and comparable to the task at hand. I had been academically prepared, holding a B.A, M.Sc and a D. Min degree. I felt strongly that I had the burning of the Holy Spirit, which accompanied my learning, thus allowing me to deliver powerful prophetic charismatic sermons, hence creating dynamic preaching. But I had a problem. I did not know how to wait on The Lord.

Let me confess that I had preached many sermons on waiting on The Lord. I had counseled many on how blessed it was to wait on The Lord and be of good courage, but now that the spotlight was on me as pastor of a new work, waiting seemed to take a new dimension. I just could not sit and wait on God to take His time to tell me when to move, how to move why to move. So I paid the price.

I am happy that you have been inspired to read this book. I trust that you will question the many philosophical differences that will be raised, only to agree with me that some precious time has been dedicated to research and Theology, particularly as it relates to an understanding of a Teleological and Ontological God.

Maybe there have been times when you failed to wait on God, and you have suffered defeat as I have in my Ministry. Perhaps you did it ignorantly or maybe because of anxiety, and you have ended up paying a great price as I did. Let us together discover the power that is ours to enjoy when we wait on God.

Yes If waiting is your problem, I want you to see how that problem can be solved with the Word of God. Far too often the waiting time is due to our not walking upright according to The Word of God:

> "For The Lord God is a sun and shield: The Lord will give grace and glory: no good thing will He withhold from them that walk up rightly."

> Psalm 84:11

CHAPTER ONE

Is Waiting an Art or Science?

How can the act of waiting be classified?

There are three ways it may be interpreted.

Dictionary.com seemed to inspire me the most with its definition.

1. To remain inactive or in a state of repose, as until something expected happens.
2. To postpone or delay something or to be postponed or delayed.
3. To look forward eagerly.

As to its definition, I believe that the least accepted definition of waiting, is that of," Looking forward eagerly. "It is that definition we will use. Later on in this book, you will see why this has come to be my choice. Is it an Art or is it Science? How should we go about classifying it?

Let us begin our quest to establish the act of waiting as being an act of eagerness.

Is waiting an art or is it a science?

Science covers the broad field of human knowledge concerned with facts held together by principles or rules. Nothing can be classified or related to Science, unless it is backed by factual evidence, and certain rules have been adhered thereto.

Chemistry is a science, because it follows set rules and formulae. Mathematic is a science because it follows established principles. No one can become a chemist, unless he understands the formula for certain mixtures.

When something is considered relating to the Arts, it is, in a broad sense, a skill in the making or doing of something. For example, teachers use the term Language Arts to refer to the related skills of reading, writing, spelling and speaking.

Everyone who is able to write, read, spell or speak, had to have within, a quiet skill waiting to be ignited through being taught that skill. Hence, some persons are better at it than others. Perhaps this is because they applied themselves more willingly, or more aggressively, to the skill. It did not happen without help but it existed all along.

I repeat, in as much as both are areas which one must apply self to attain success, the Arts is something that one has within but needing to be exercised. This is not to be with a scientist. He has to be able to apply facts and rules to be successful.

All an individual has to do is to be around someone speaking a particular language, and if interested, they will be able to speak it; if they are able to watch someone forming figures or letters, not very long, if they are interested, will be able to write ; if there is a desire for one to read, all that is needed is to listen and observe the sound made by each letter, by the one reading. If there is an interest, the Arts will trigger in us, which is innately present within. Everyone is not born to be a chemist, but everyone is born to speak.

Therefore, I honestly believe that waiting is an Art. You need no formula to do it, you just look at how other people act, how they would pause, and stand still when there is need to do so. If they have a relationship with God, that great teacher the pedagogue will show up. They would then say, let me think. To wait affords the individual to participate in personal reflections. Usually it is from a historical perspective.

You just need to understand why they waited. When things look dim, they know what waiting will do. It places them in a position of being able to look forward eagerly.

Well some might say that the Arts and the Sciences are similar in that some form of instructions are dispensed.

They may be similar because they are both designed to help individuals in the way forward.

They may be similar because they both predict experiences.

3

Art is like the binding force of Science

On the other side they cannot be compared.

Science studies God's creation.

Art admires and enjoys God's creation

Science is the practice of investigation based on hypothesis which is derived from observation.

Art is a combination of age long events of proven things.

Art is not about invention, it's all about historical perspectives that have already been proven and given permission by time to occur.

So then if waiting is an act of eager anticipation, this cannot be something that is formulated, but rather, that which is innate and ready to step into full gear, when time permits. Therein lies the reason for my decision that waiting is an Art, because it hinges on the matter of time.

So then, let it be considered as of the Arts. If so, it is therefore related with such subjects as : Dance, History, Music, English Language and Literature, Business Studies and Religious studies, just to name a few.

Arts therefore represents an outlet of human expressions, usually influenced by culture and driven by human creative impulse. The art of waiting is a show of human expressions, that is usually influenced by our culture, and driven by how and when we wish things to happen.

When one sincerely and truly waits, he waits in eager anticipation that in time, something will happen.

Psalm 130:6 is recorded by The New American Standard Bible like this: "I wait patiently for The Lord more than watchman wait for the morning; Indeed more than watchmen wait for the morning." (NASB)

No one has to teach a watchman how to wait. There is no formula that he could use to hurry up the time in waiting. It's just the eagerness in seeing the sun burst forth, to herald the arrival of a new day that has taught him the art.

CHAPTER TWO

The Biblical Pronouncement on Wait

Having established, as best possible, for you to appreciate, the point that the act of waiting should be viewed as an Art; and that the culture surrounding it should be that of eager anticipation, I hasten to my next point:

The Biblical Pronouncement on Waiting.

Pronouncement refers to having an authoritative word.

Is it an established fact that all the persons in the Bible who had reasons to wait on God, did it with eagerness? Was their waiting culture caged in eager anticipation? If that were not to be, what was it like, and how did God respond to their request? Better yet, what may we learn from their experiences?

First of all, this chapter wants us to scripturally hear what God, through His written word, has to say about the act of waiting on Him.

In the Decalogue, the very first book of Moses, there are recordings of God speaking into existence, the magnificent creation of the heaven and the earth. He does it within the confines of time, as we now know it now to be. God made all things within six days.

The Book of Genesis Chapter 1: 1 - 5, from The Holy Book, in the King James Version, translated out of the Original Tongues (and with Previous Translations, diligently compared and revised), says this:

"1. In the beginning God created the heaven and the earth.
2. And the earth was without form, and void; and darkness was upon the face of the deep. And the spirit of God moved upon the face of the waters.
3. And God said, Let there be light: and there was light,
4. And God saw the light, that it was good: and God divided the night from the darkness.
5. And God called the light Day, and the darkness he called Night.
6. And the evening and the morning were the first day."

As one continues to read the Book of Genesis regarding the story of creation, it is evident that the first point God teaches us about waiting is simply this. Time and the act of waiting plays a very important part within the functions of human existence. Simply stated, everything surrounding the existence and continuation of the life of man, came to be, through the process of time. There was a waiting period of no less than a morning and an evening.

In as much as we have developed into an "instant now" generation, God wants us to understand that there will always be some things and some times which He, The Omnipotent, Omniscient, Omnipresent God will take His time, at performing.

It does not matter what it is and how important it may be to us, there will always be somethings that will be inclusive in the matter of waiting.

We will have to wait on the birth of a child. We will have to wait for crops to grow. We will have to wait for night to follow day, and the list goes on.

Just consider for a moment, God allows, with all the power He has at His disposal, of being able to operate without the boundaries of time; to create, a brand new world, with time and patience uniquely connected in the act of waiting, and to complete creation through just speaking it into existence in six days.

God determines the "when."

Herein stands our first Pronouncement regarding the matter of waiting. It does not matter how important or how urgent a matter may be, God determines the "when" it shall become.

So what will be our reward if we allow ourselves to go through God's established process, by waiting on His move?

Well, the result of God using time to create the heaven and the earth, beginning in the first morning, by creating light from darkness, and completing it all in the evening? God said that all was good. Expect God to say, it's good, if that which requires a time to wait, is given that privilege.

Trust and Obey while Waiting.

Our second incident regarding having to wait, is recorded in the book of 1 Samuel 13. In this incident we see God giving specific command through his Prophet to a King which resulted in the testing of his ability to wait on Him. The Biblical lesson in this particular incident is "Trust and Obey while Waiting.» To wait truly teaches one how to obey the voice of God or His representatives.

Samuel our professor for this principle says to King Saul in 1 Samuel 13:13:

> "And Samuel said to Saul, Thou hast done foolishly: thou hast not kept the commandment of The Lord thy God, which He commanded thee."

Saul is at war with the Philistines.

He was gradually losing his fighting men. The men of Israel were in a strait. They were distressed. His soldiers were hiding in caves, in the thickets, in rocks, in high places and in pits. Many of them went over Jordan to the land of Gad and Gilead.

This is what faced Saul. Plus, the man of God whose job it was to bless the troop before the battle, was seven days late. No battle was to begin without the man of God present to offer up a sacrifice. But the man of God was seven days late, and the king was losing his fighting men.

The Bible records that Saul took it upon himself to perform the sacrifice that a priest would do. He was in a desperate situation, and there was no voice from God or His representative, so he did what he was not to do. Time was past, and he was tired of waiting, while watching his army fall apart.

The interesting thing about this scenario is that verse ten in the same book and chapter records thus:

And it came to pass, that as soon as he had made an end of offering the burnt offering, behold, Samuel came.

Trust and Obey while waiting!

What a lesson.

It is true that all lessons must end with a test. You will only know what you understood from the professor, when you passed his test.

Waiting teaches us the hard lesson in the fact that waiting is futile if there exists no semblance of trust and obedience.

Not to wait will definitely reveal that much will be lost through not trusting while waiting.

Saul's incident is a striking example of this. Samuel told King Saul what was his to gain had he waited. God would have established Saul's kingdom upon Israel forever.

Now that he had failed to wait on the move of God, Samuel told him that his kingdom shall not continue; The Lord had replaced him with a man after His own heart.

It is very expensive not to wait on God, particularly when instructed so to do.

Waiting travels with good company.

The third Biblical Pronouncement for our consideration is that according to Bible, waiting travels along with some good company.

The authors of the Old Testament Books of Isaiah and The Psalms, chime in to speak to this topic.

Isaiah 40:31,

"But they that wait upon The Lord, shall renew their strength; they shall mount up with wings as angels; they shall run, and not be weary; and they shall walk, and not faint."

Waiting upon The Lord, renews one strength in such ways that will be liken unto the strong wings of an eagle, permitting them to be able to fly high tirelessly; having the ability liken unto an athlete to run any race without being discouraged due to the lack of strength; walk any distance and any road and not be tempted to give up due to the distance still to travel.

Psalm 27:14.

"Wait on The Lord: be of good courage, and He shall strengthen thine heart: wait, I say, on The Lord."

This type of waiting speaks to a determined spirit that will not quit.

I wish to point out that there has been a poor interpretation of what the Psalmist meant when saying to his readers to wait on The Lord.

Many have been tempted to think that waiting on The Lord means to stop all activity, be very still, clear our minds and place all attention on God, with a blank look.

This has come about from the idea of pausing or of being still, which might describe someone who is waiting.

Brethren, one can pause without waiting. The concept of waiting is actually very different from what I have described.

The Hebrew word translated wait is "qavah" meaning to wait, to look for, to hope and to expect.

Being idle, still, or empty, is not the same as waiting.

Doing nothing, seeking nothing, is not necessarily waiting.

If we are waiting, we are waiting for something, something we expect. Waiting implies eager anticipation, great expectation.

It is good to reflect on John 5:3 for some help. We read that many persons who were sick of varying diseases, waited at the pool, excitedly anticipating that the next troubling of the water, would be their long expected miracle. This waiting ends in being blessed immensely.

Psalm 40:1

"I waited patiently for The Lord; and He inclined unto me, and heard my cry."

There is nothing so comforting to babies who as soon as they open their mouth in search of attention, feel the strong, soft loving hands of a mother reaching down in the crib and rescuing them.

Even more so if their cry was due to some pain or loneliness, and perhaps have been with them for some while, that some concerned adult reaches in and rescues them.

The lesson to be learned from waiting according to this Psalmist is that the period of waiting may produce a feeling of loneliness, pain, rejection, hunger for physical attention, and the desire to be lifted out of your present situation.

The Psalmist said in verse two of that same chapter: "He brought me up also out of an horrible pit, out of my miry clay, and set my feet upon a rock, and established my goings.

And he hath put a new song in my mouth, even praise unto our God: many shall see it, and fear, and shall trust in The Lord."

13

We are being encouraged to wait by this Psalmist, for he wishes us to see the rewards to be received.

However, he implies at the beginning of his psalm that the place of waiting will not always be a position of comfort. This must be understood. In fact that is why waiting is not a coveted condition for one to want to be in for any length of time.

The Psalmist describes it as liken unto being in a horrible pit, with miry clay to stand in.

But after a period of crying, under such uncomfortable circumstance, God will bend over to where we are crying to deliver us out of it.

Notice how he does it:

1. He gives us something to stand on, a firm hope or belief.
2. He gives new instructions on the way forward, accompanied with new directions.
3. He makes us excited about where we are now, and where we are going, by giving us a new song.
4. Now we will have a testimony along with a praise, that will be the envy of all who hear it.
5. They shall see me delivered and shall respect me, and shall want to trust in The Lord.

All that I have shared with you regarding the subject, cannot be seen as exhaustive. There is more Biblical Pronouncement on the subject of waiting.

CHAPTER THREE

Psychological Effects from Waiting

What is psychology?

The word "psychology" comes from the Greek word psyche meaning "breath, spirit, soul."

Psychology has never been a clear cut discipline. To help understand the ambiguity surrounding Psychology, I wish to look at a few definitions:

1. The scientific study of people, the mind and behaviour.
2. The study of behavior and mental processes.

Since the word behaviour or behaviourism appears in both definitions, what then does behaviour refer to within the context of psychology?

Behavior refers to the manner in which one behaves or act. Behaviourism refers to the belief that one's behavior can be measured, trained and changed.

It is a theory of learning based upon the idea that all behaviors are acquired through conditioning.

So what is psychology?

It is both an applied and academic science that studies the human mind and behaviour.

In this field, a professional practitioner or researcher is called a psychologist and can be classified as a social behavioral or cognitive scientist. They try as best possible to understand the role of mental functions in individuals and social behaviour, while also exploring the physiological and biological processes that underlie cognitive functions and behaviours.

Thus psychology is confronted with trying to find out why are children stubborn; why do some people become addicted to drugs or gambling; how do you help an abused child?

All of those difficult and challenging questions, the many psychology schools of thought are trying to address.

Psychology is truly a broad discipline which seeks to analyze the human mind.

Having said all the above, let us now pursue the thought that waiting can be viewed as a mind game. Let's investigate thoroughly how one's mind is affected as a result of having to wait, particularly for an inordinate period of time.

I truly believe, without a doubt that waiting can and does affect one's mind, hence one's social behaviour. For example, there is no argument against the fact that waiting, in a practical sense, can be frustrating, demoralizing, agonizing and aggravating, time consuming and incredibly expensive.

Just reflect for a moment. Remind yourself of perhaps having to stand on a line to pay a bill, perform some type of banking needs or even waiting on an elevator or a doctor for service.

If you are trying to conduct business within a limited break from your job, and the teller or cashier shows no interest in expediting your transaction, you become nervous and frustrated.

If the bank is filled to capacity, and there seem to be hardly any teller on duty, you become annoyed and angry.

If you have an appointment with a dentist, for some type of dental procedure, and others are served before you are, this creates a feeling of being overlooked, and you really become filled with disgust.

I am quite sure that you can very well associate your emotional feelings with any or all of the above.

So then it stands to reason that waiting does affect one psychologically, as those areas mentioned are more mental than physical.

Psychologically speaking, here are a few very interesting comments and observations showing how waiting affects one psychologically.

Occupied time, feels shorter than unoccupied time.

Anxiety makes wait seem longer. Uncertain waits appear much longer than known finite waits.

Unexplained waits seem longer than explained waits.

Unfair waits appear longer than equitable waits.

Solo waits feel longer than group waits.

These examples establish the fact that waiting truly affects the mind, and can pose a very negative response.

So how can we as Christians avoid waiting that might cause us to display the wrong kind of behaviour, particularly when having to wait on God?

I do believe, without a shadow of a doubt, we can control it by simply thinking positively.

The best way to think positively is to constantly commune with God, through the medium of prayer and praise.

The New Century Version records 1 Cor 14:15 like this:

"So what should I do? I will pray with my spirit, but I will also pray with my mind. I will sing with my spirit, but I will also sing with my mind." (NCV)

If that is the case, this leads me into the subject of Mind over Matter.

Mind over matter was a phrase popularized during the 1960, and 1970s, that was originally used in reference to paranormal phenomena such as psychokinesis. This means having the ability to move matter around with your mind, without making any physical contact.

This school of thought believes that the mind is more powerful than all the matter in the universe and can accomplish anything that can be imagined.

Mind over matter is also described as will power. This is what one sees at work, as an athlete or a boxer, whose body is paining beyond measure, continues the task to the very end.

Lots of researchers have proven that the power of the mind, can accomplish anything in the universe, if one can control the thought patterns of his/her mind.

One can make goals come to past in a very short time, by constantly thinking about them, thus reducing the amount of time spent in waiting.

So the concept of mind over matter science, emphasizes the fact that anything is possible if you can train your mind to function in a particular way. This thought needs to be considered very carefully, and must be supported strongly by scripture.

If a Christian ascribes to this manner of operating, this could say to them that there should not be any waiting time for things they wish to accomplish, provided their mind wants it to be. Hence, Christians who are not taught correctly from the Word of God, could find themselves, depending on speaking things into existence, void of approaching God through the medium of prayer.

Let us search the scripture as it relates to our mind, the mind of God and how to understand how it functions.

1 Corinth. 2:16

"For who hath known the mind of The Lord, that he may instruct him? But we have the mind of Christ."

Romans 12:1-2

"I beseech you therefore brethren, by the mercies of God, that ye present your bodies a living sacrifice, holy, acceptable unto God, which is your reasonable service.

And be not conformed to this world: but be ye transformed by the renewing of your mind, that ye may prove what is good, and acceptable, and perfect, will of God."

Philippians 2:5

Let this mind be in you, which was also in Christ Jesus:

Get the mind of Christ and all of its benefits as is recorded in Philippians 2:5.

Have you ever wondered how this is possible?

As previously stated, God created the human mind as a combination of conscious and unconscious processes (thought) of the brain that directs our mental and physical behaviour. Our thought influence our actions. So if we want to act like Christ, we must also think like Him.

There are many other benefits to having the mind of Christ. (Col 2:3)

1. We will come to the full knowledge of the mystery of God
2. We will have life and peace (Rom 8:6)
3. We will have the will of God for our lives. (Hebrew 13:21)
4. We will know that God wants us to come and reason with Him.

Not having the mind of Christ will cause us to live a life of disobedience and rebellion.

Rebellion is a refusal to seek His mind in all things. We can never obtain the mind of Christ by relying on our own reasoning.

1 Peter 1:13

Wherefore gird up the loins of your mind, be sober, and hope to the end for the grace that is to be brought unto you at the revelation of Jesus Christ.

2 Timothy 1:7

For God hath not given us the spirit of fear; but of power, and of love, and of a sound mind.

Yes the mind is a very powerful, tool that God has given to us. Therefore we are admonished to let our mind be that of Christ. It can create 'reality' in a sense, because what we think determines who we will become, and what we can achieve. It can make us successful or cause us to become beggars.

If we put our minds to succeed, through Christ, we can overcome many obstacles, including physical ones.

Nevertheless, there are still those who prefer to remain on the purely physical plane, refusing to believe that the mind is separate from the brain and that while the latter acts like a useful computer, it certainly has no power over our bodies, and more certainly no influence on our desires.

Whether that statement is totally or partly correct, I have shown you from the Word of God, that the mind is a powerful tool, and should be allowed to be influenced, controlled by the Holy Spirit.

If this is not to be, Satan will move in and make use of it to do his work. Perhaps that is where such things as omen, black magic and the like, have come to exist.

Lest we lose the purpose for which this chapter is all about, permit me to do a brief review. What are the psychological effects from waiting?

We have shown where waiting effects one's time and mind, resulting in one's social behaviour being negatively affected. When this happens, the one affected, will begin to respond in an unseemly manner to his/her family, friends and those on the job.

If the people and circumstances that influence our mental processing are godly, they will find it easier to deal with the matter of waiting on God.

If it is a spiritual matter, and the mind of God does not exist, there is that possibility of losing contact with both church and God.

Do not permit having to wait on God for anything and for any length of time, to go by unchecked, resulting in the spirit of negativity blossoming.

Be sure that there exist a clear understanding on why you are waiting, and whether you are waiting in the correct frame of mind.

Please remember, waiting on God, is not just standing idly by, but being busy, having eager anticipation.

Put you mind to work every time you begin to think, permitting a constant flow of positive words from the Holy Spirit.

Finally, be encouraged by the many saints who waited on a promise from God, never giving up.

Job declares that he will wait until his change comes.

Abraham died looking for a city which God had promised him.

I close by referring to a strong question made by Moses in his first book, Gen 18:25 "......shall not the Judge of all the earth do right?

CHAPTER FOUR

How Do You Wait On God?

Waiting on God is the special process through which The Lord causes our eyes to turn to Him for help in time of need.

It is a crucial step in which our dependence upon God grows. It is a time in which we do not have resources, answers, or direction. Instead we are often confused, poor, broken and limited.

Our hope is focused on what happens after that season of humility, where we will experience a period of God's blessing.

The Psalmist joins our discussion and proclaims these words:

> "I waited patiently for The Lord; and He inclined
> unto me, and heard my cry." Psalm 40:1

Reference has been made to this verse of scripture, in previous discussions, but I feel compelled to return to it again, particularly in this chapter. I do this because there is a word which I feel must be explained in order for you my reader to appreciate my approach to this topic, and why I used such an opening statement.

The word is patiently. It is an adverb of manner, telling how something happens. It speaks to the manner in which the wait being done by David is conducted.

The phrase, "waiting on God" seem to have originated with David. He not only experienced great difficulty in his life but discovered that he could wait upon God for help.

At the very beginning of this chapter, the Psalmist David describes to us the sad state in which he found himself, waiting on God.

He was as one in a horrible pit. Additionally, it was an area consisting of swampy, deep soft mud. He describes the ground as being filled with miry clay, slowly pulling him down. In the midst of it all, he was crying unto The Lord.

The interesting thing was that he was there waiting patiently for The Lord. He was not complaining about his condition, he was there crying, and waiting patiently for The Lord to deliver him.

Then the Psalmist records that The Lord heard his cry, and bought him out.

Please note what preceded him being brought out?

First, The Lord inclined Himself, then He brought him out. This is anthropomorphic language, applying the actions of a man to God.

Perhaps if the Psalmist were not waiting patiently, and crying loud enough for God to hear him, there would not have been a need for God to bend down to him.

Brethren this is not to indicate that unless our cry is loud and long, God does not hear it. What I do understand it to mean is exactly what I mentioned earlier as to what the results from waiting.

We see this lesson being strongly taught at the death and resurrection of Lazarus.

In this incident, Jesus says that as a result of Lazarus death, God will cause Lazarus' friends and family to witness the awesome power of God so that His Father would be glorified.

Waiting upon God protects us, deepens our trust in Him, forces us to seek His ways and bring Him the most glory.

They are the times when The Lord is testing us, for us to know whether we are really seeking Him and His ways.

The second lesson Jesus taught:

Jesus said that as a result of Lazarus death, it will cause many doubters to believe in the power of God.

The longer we wait on God, the more we will suffer. The more we suffer, many more people will observe our condition and even hear our cry. Hence at the end of this season, your testimony will be clearly understood by many, resulting in many who doubted God to be converted. They would have watched you patiently waiting on God.

There is definitely a place for one to exhibit patience while waiting, because of the results to be gained.

Yes it is a known fact that far too often, we would find ourselves resigned to waiting patiently on many events, especially if we know without a doubt, that it will occur, with the passing of time.

So what does it mean to wait patiently?

Patiently is defined as, "bearing or enduring pain, trouble etc without complaining or losing self control."

The Thesaurus has it associated with such adjectives as, assiduously, devotedly, doggedly, enduringly faithfully, forbearingly.

So, what does it mean to wait patiently on God?

Having regard for those mentioned, here are some ideas on what it means.

1. As a waiter in a restaurant, who attends to the customer.

He does this with pride, permitting himself where possible to always be within hearing or seeing distance of his customer. He does not stop serving until the customer pays him, and perhaps, gives him a tip.

He is always conscious that the customer is king, and he, is his servant. He makes it his business to be happy and active as he serves. He knows that poor service from him, could cost him his job.

That is what waiting patiently on God is all about.

2. Wait patiently as an active person would do who has great expectations.

Any person who looks forward expecting something from someone whom he has reposed great trust, does not wait carelessly for that which he knows will soon be his to enjoy.

He waits in active anticipation.

He begins to prepare himself for it's arrival, as well as prepare his surroundings. If it's a car, he begins to build a garage. If it's a house, he is busy shopping for furniture placing things on lay-away. If it's a new born, adequate space etc is being looked into, and the list goes on.

No one who expects something to happen waits around and does nothing.

A child of God should have great expectations. This is because he serves a God who has made him many great promises, and who has proven to be faithful to his promises.

3. Wait patiently as a person who looks forward to, while making preparations for, the day and time of the celebrated festive days.

It does not matter or how long it may seem that the celebration of Christmas Day, Halloween, Easter, New Years Day, or the arrival time for a birthday, drags on. When the day arrives the fun that accompanies it, is more than compensates for the patience required to wait for the grand affair.

There just seem to exist that consoling fact that, they will come, and regardless of how long it takes, there is nothing that we can do to hasten their arrival. We know that they will arrive, and that the only thing that will stop us from seeing them would be death.

When we wait for God to do something that He is well able to perform, we must relax and wait.

Tell yourself that the arrival of what God has promised you, is more sure than Christmas Day, which we wait three hundred and sixty-five say to arrive, doing nothing to help it along.

4. Wait patiently as one with confidence, not doubting, possessing a sure and certain hope.

Hope is expected possibilities. It is that which stays with you to the very end, and even beyond. It is confidence one dies with, which circumstances cannot deter, and situations dare not alter. It goes beyond, "what if" to "whatever." This is usually the final wait.

I have discovered from Job's experience, recorded in Chapter 17 and onwards, that this man of God had lost hope, yes he did. It was not that he had given up totally. What Job found himself doing was turning loose all physical things of worth and value, but locking on to things spiritual. That is what hope is all about. Not turning loose everything, but getting rid of some things. Job tries to explain this to his three friends.

Job says, in Chapter 19 and onward, that as a result of his tests and trials, he saw all that he had hoped for, in this world, dropping with him in the grave.

He is not hopeless, but his hope was not where his friends would have it to be. As for his hope, the hope which comforted and supported him, it could not be seen by the visible eyes. It was like something out of sight that he hopes for, and was eternal.

Job said that he was seeing things that will abide forever.

How do you wait on God?

Wait patiently wait hopefully.

Wait expectantly.

Wait actively.

Wait on God as one that is timeless in nature. By so doing, not placing a time limit on Him. There is a saying that He may not come when you want Him, but he'll come just on time.

St Paul in his writing to the Corinthian Brethren, admonishes them to be "steadfast, unmovable, always abounding in the work of The Lord, forasmuch as ye know that your labour is not in vain in The Lord." 1Corinth. 15:58

That's how you wait on God.

Do you believe God will give you the desires of your heart if you wait patiently on Him? I strongly believe that He will.

I challenge you to do that. I know that waiting for Him can be painful. I know that you might become discouraged, wondering if God will answer your prayers. Or, you could become angry when you see Him blessing others with the very thing you would like to have.

Just expect Him to come through for you.

CHAPTER FIVE

Waiting Signs

Some years ago, when Disney Land was very new, and the desire to take young people to it was exciting, I along with a group of adults from our church, took up the challenge.

We agreed to fly to Miami, Florida, rent vans, get a few road maps, and drive to Disney World in Orlando, Florida.

I must confess that I did not expect the drive from Miami to Orlando to be so very long, particularly being a native of the small island of New Providence, Bahamas. On this little island, no place was very far from each other.

So it was in the late 1990s, we left Miami to begin our journey to Disney Land. There was total excitement in our vans as we travelled the long highways and interstates on our route.

After a few hours had gone by, along with many restless moments sitting in the vans, there came a question, from among the passengers, "Are we there yet."

My response to them was that they begin to look and read the signs along the way. Signs would tell them if we are far away, nearby or there, and so sadly they began to read every sign hoping that eventually they would read that final sign that would indicate that they were entering, "Disney World."

This chapter talks about signs, those which should help individuals to know if they are on the right course in waiting on God.

A sign is any object, act or gesture used to convey an idea, a desire, information, a meaning, or a command. To wait in this chapter, refers to an act conveying a desire.

I have been led, as I wrote this book, to study the history regarding the origin of signs. I have found the history of signs to be extremely interesting, particularly how it relates to our topic. Like most inherited conveniences, we don't much notice the importance of signs until we don't have them around.

It is a fact that signs help make us move around or into areas intelligently. They provide a universal symbology for direction, warning, order, and measurement.

I have been informed that as people became civilized and began to travel via trade routes, the Egyptians were among the earliest civilization to use road markers. The Greeks and Romans carried on the tradition with the Romans making what we might consider the first ones of terra colia, a brownish red earthy material

I have discovered that the Early Christians were one of the first religious body to use signs, adopting the fish and the cross as a guide to where their churches were meeting, although pagan religions had long used idols as symbols of their temples as well.

From that brief history of signs, there now exist three points which connect us to the topic," Waiting Signs. "Therefore, to truly deal with our topic, we must supply information for the following questions.

How does one know when he is truly waiting on God?

What if I am doing all that I believe is right and proper, but perhaps I am not doing it correctly?

Are there specific signs I should look forward to, that will tell me when to stop, when to go, where to exit, where to enter, how fast to go, how slow to proceed, when I am nearing my destination etc?

In not appearing to be authoritative on this subject, I do believe that there are specific signs which help us in our quest to wait patiently on God. We have learned from the history of signs that certain signs speak to particular needs.

If we are waiting on God, it must be for a particular reason. Therefore certain signs should indicate that particular need. The only way we would know how to send the right signal, we must be familiar with the Word of God. Our answer is located in The Bible, which is our manual for our life

No kind of instrument made by man exists without a manual. It does not matter how large or small it may be. Whether it is electrical or mechanical in its function, or both, there exists a manual with proper instructions for the maintenance and operation of the machine. The owner of all equipment will do well to familiarize himself/herself with the manual. Should anything go wrong, the manual is there to offer the necessary information to correct the malady.

Such should be the position, the Bible holds, in the lives of every Christian. That is our first sign which needs to be very obvious in our lives, in our quest to wait patiently on God. Are we studying the Word of God? How well do we know our manual?

We have learned from history, that signs were first used by The Early Church, to assist in connecting Christian communities with each other. The sign that was made was in the form of a fish, which indicated that a church met at that location.

Signs later became a universal symbology for direction, warning, and order. With the use of signs, it improved communication as to where they would assemble.

The main purpose for The Early Church meeting was to learn more about their newly found way of worship, and for daily fellowship through the breaking of Bread.

As a child of God, one of our waiting signs should indicate a fresh new way we worship God together, and fellowship with each other. The word of God must be studied and adhered to if we are going to wait patiently, doing it God's way, while embracing a fresh way in worshipping Him, and fellowshipping with the Brethren.

St Paul tells Timothy that if he wishes to be approved of God, he must study the Word of a God. No approval will be granted in anything he needed, without knowing the Word.

History also records that one of the purposes for signs, was to help society, move around intelligently, avoiding any collision. This should say to us that the signs we send out while waiting on God, must be clear. Unless our signs are being interpreted correctly by those around us, they can be misleading.

Nothing is so harmful as that of a misleading sign to a road user. A good example would be that of an arrow on a road sign that have been inadvertently shifted due to strong winds. It has been turned in the opposite direction, therefore persons not familiar with the area would go west as opposed to east.

A sign stating exit instead of entrance, could cause an accident.

It is a must that signs be clear at all times and not some times.

Signs are supposed to provide a universal symbology, thus making us move around intelligently, so should be the waiting signs we send forward. Take time to intelligently share with those you consider very close to you. Failing to do that, could lead to a serious spiritual collision.

Finally, let us remember those pressing concerns which were raised initially, for our consideration. How can you as a believer, thrive in the midst of a painful season of waiting?

Here are a few strong reminders.

1. Be honest, don't fake a happy face. I am not telling you to wear a sad melancholy face, but permit persons to know that all is not well, but there is hope for a better tomorrow. (Psalm 77: 1-2 & 62:8)
2. Trust that God has a purpose for his delay. Remember that God is working behind the scene. (Psalm 84: 11-12)
3. Ask God to supply your needs. (1Timothy 6:17 & Matt.7:7-8)
4. Prepare for God's answer. In preparing, you accomplish two things: you are demonstrating faith that God will fulfill your desire, and you are preparing for success. (John 10:10)
5. Be thankful and content. (Philippians 4:11-12)
6. Serve The Lord joyfully. (Psalm 100)

Brethren I admonish you to be very careful of the signs you send forth while waiting on God. Make sure they are clear.

CHAPTER SIX

Time Will Make
Or Break You

How is one's mind affected as a result of having to wait, particularly if for an inordinate period of time?

It appears as if today, it has become very easy for some Christians to give up on God, when the tests they are enduring become long and severe. On the other hand, there are other Christians who have become more determined to keep on going, despite what is happening to them, resulting in their faith growing stronger, in the midst of their adversities.

To one group, time appeared to be their greatest enemy, causing them to become weak and eventually succumbing to its pressure; while to the other, time has made them stronger. To them, it was like having to spend long hours, like an athlete training for a fight, in a GYM, having to spend quality time building muscles while loosing unnecessary weight. So, having to endure, while training, strengthened their resolve making them to not give up easily.

What determined the deciding factor between those two groups, who started out with the same determined spirit, and apparently the same depth of spiritual growth, but only one to truly endure?

I don't believe that the answer, for such a question can be determined by just one being able to endure through holding on. What I would like to believe is that it is based on the ability of one to endure, thus increasing the strength of the individual, along with something else. I believe that something is the fact of "Time", understanding it philosophically.

So what is time, and it's relationship to one's past, present, and future?

How do we experience it?

Can we really understand it?

These along with many other questions, will be discussed in this chapter.

Let us begin firstly, looking at the matter of "time."

Time truly affects us in many ways. We use it; we abuse it; we enjoy it; we fear it. Time encompasses both fascination and mystery. That is why we would often hear persons say such things as," he arrived just in the nick of time," or "I most certainly had a great time."

Time is often described as an ever flowing stream. It is quite appropriate to use the word time to talk about at least three different phenomena, all quite distinct though usually confused in our minds. Therefore I have decided that there are three types of time to which we must look at. This is important for us to be able to understand which time is being considered as having the ability to either make us or break our spiritual walk with God.

The first to be discussed is clock time or chronological time, called Chronos.

This type of time is usually portrayed using a picture of an old, wise man with a long, grey beard, to whom we commonly refer to as Father Time. Chronos refers to sequential time, a moment of indeterminate time in which everything happens.

Chronos deals with time that is chronological or sequential in nature.

When referring to the age of or aging of something, the time given is Chronos. It is quantitative.

A very interesting point about Chronos or clock time is that it probably has nothing whatsoever to do with time. Clocks measure space. Clocks are designed to work in conjunction with the sun's motion. Therefore we try to synchronize both the sun and the clock, implying our understanding that real time is in the operation.

However what we are really doing is working events and not synchronizing time. Chronos time is marked and named. "Two o'clock," and "Three-thirty o'clock." These designations are "of the clock," meaning they belong to the clock, which is the great measurer of Chronos time. We strap small clocks to our wrists and call them "watches," because with them we can watch Chronos time coming and going

A second kind of time is subjective time, or experiential time. This is perhaps the only temporal phenomenon of which we have any clear conception. This time which is also called Psychological time is our individual experience of the continuum of our consciousness. Consciousness is time. When we are asleep, or unconscious, time is nonexistent to us, but it begins the moment we regain consciousness. It is no small wonder why, as soon as we awake, we would gaze at a clock, or ask the question of what time is it.

The third description of time is called Kairos.

Physicists say that time is the 4th dimension. If that is true, it makes understanding time a bit tricky for us, mired as we are in a 3-dimensional world.

But we experience time as a single moment we call the present.

What I'm saying is, comprehending time in its fullness is beyond us.

The Greeks however, understood that time was too complex to be contained in only one word, so they had two words for time: Chronos and Kairos. They were caught in the same 3 dimensions that hold us, so they couldn't understand time any better than we can, but I'm impressed that they made the effort. It is the kind of time that you and I are most familiar with.

James L Christian, in his book entitled,' Philosophy, the Art of Wondering, devoted a chapter to the subject 'Past/Present/Future.

In this chapter, some of the above information were listed. I feel strongly that his information relative to Saint Augustine's notes on God's Time and Ours, need to be shared.

The author writes, "Saint Augustine's concept of time is conditioned by his theological presuppositions. God created time, along with creation.

Since God created time, He existed before time, He will exist after time, and therefore He exists outside time. There was no time before God created it. In the mind of God, there is no before or after, there is only a now.

In God's experience, all events occur simultaneously. This is to say that all past and all future events exist together in God's present."

No wonder His plea to man for salvation has always been, 'come now and let us reason, saith The Lord (Isaiah 1:18).

We human beings experience the present, remember the past, anticipate the future; but God is not limited by our human time.

It is not correct to say, as some preachers do, that there are really two times; God's time and man's time. This is not so because man exist in time, but God is timeless. His is "kairos."

Kairos time is therefore referred to as, "The Lord's Time. Kairos time is to man, that moment when change is possible.

It's a moment when something happens.

It is qualitative in nature.

It is that moment of opportunity, which may happen with a passing instant, when an opening appears which must be driven through with force, if success is to be achieved.

The statement, time will make or break you" refers to which time? I do believe that in ignorance, many see it as kairos, the Lord's time. This chapter will take a position on which time is being referred to.

Let's begin our final investigation.

Let us first understand what is meant by 'to make' or 'to break'

Webster agrees with me that:

To make means to cause something to come into existence, usually that something would have never existed prior to it being made.

To make may also refer to one being successful at a particular venture. This can mean that one has made it up the ladder of success. His time struggling with, or planning about, have finally paid off. They have made it.

The word break refers to some kind of action being done. It lends itself to the possibility of something or someone being destroyed. Sometimes when something is broken, it is no longer able to serve it's intended purpose. A good example of it is a glass that has dropped to the ground, and is no longer of any use.

There are times when relationships between a man and a woman find itself broken. When this takes place, very seldom are they mended. Even if the relationship is repaired, it might not be as strong and caring as it once was.

It is believed that To be broken by time has similar consequences. It becomes very hard for a Christian to redeem lost time resulting from a faith that has been broken. A broken faith speaks of the results one experiences after believing in someone or trusting strongly for something, for a long time, only to see that which he/she had hoped for or believed in, failed.

A broken faith can come about as a result of time, through seeing a loved one suffer for a long period, and to eventually die, even after much prayer and fasting were offered up.

One's faith could be broken if time persists concerning a special request, and you are able to see others being blessed with the same things you have been fasting, praying and seeding about.

Time plays a constant role in the relationship between a person and his/her God. It can help or it can hurt. It is something no human can exist without in this world. But is time really responsible for our hurts and disappointment?

If so, which time should we hold responsible for such brokenness? Is it Chronos, kairos or psychological time?

The opening statement speaks about two Christian groups and how time makes them operate differently towards their God. This then is leading me to believe that the time in question is Chronos, clock time or chronological time.

As we have studied, clock time or chronological time is called Chronos. It refers to sequential time, when one thing follows the next. We work events, performing against time as opposed to working along with Time. For example, when a concert is supposed to begin at a particular time, we work towards starting at that given time, and we continue to the end.

Time does not prepare us for the concert, it works against us, hoping that we meet our deadline. This is because time continues to move forward, like an ever flowing stream.

So time does not make things happen. Things occur because of our interacting with time.

Time does not interact, therefore it cannot make or break us.

When we see things happening to others, which we would prefer for ourselves, it's "kurios" time in action.

It's things working according to the plan of God. Since God does not plan futuristically, but presently, all which happens to a Child of God, happens now in the present.

Please remember, our present, past and future is based on Chronos. We view things happening to us either very early, on time or late, but this is not so with God. God is timeless. He operates out of the realm of time.

No wonder the songwriter penned these words, He might not come when we want Him (Chronos), but He is always right on time (kurios).

So time does not make or break us, we permit ourselves to participate in the Time game of Chronos, where we conclude when it is our time to be blessed, (kurios) and we decide whether it is either early, on time, or late. However, it all happens because of our timeless God who answers our prayers, not because it is time; not because we have been good, but because He is God. Time does not really matter with Him as it does with us.

CHAPTER SEVEN

The Weightiness of Time

"For our light affliction, which is but for a moment, worketh for us a far more exceeding and eternal weight of glory; while we look not at the things which are seen, but at the things which are not seen: for the things which are seen are temporal; but the things which are not seen are eternal."

2 Corinthian 4:17-18

A weight is something that constitutes pressure. It does not have to be made of matter, but it brings with it constant, sustained pressure, which is a type of burden.

It does not move around without help or support, it is that which must be carried. It requires supervision to be effective. It is not always visible to the naked eyes, but is experiential in the mind.

Weight is one of the many mind games humans find themselves involved with, particularly when confronted with the challenge to help lift heavy burdens off individuals. When weights become a mental attribute, it can manifest its presence through a few different means. It can operate through using psychological, sociological biological, philosophical and even spiritual avenues to impact the lives of persons. Unless this is recognized, controlled, and it's purposes made clear, the pressure it brings to bear, will do much damage to the individual Christian, within the category it operates. They will find themselves thinking the wrong thoughts; doing the wrong things; embracing the wrong feelings; and sharing the wrong views.

In as much as time was featured already in this book, in this chapter, it is not only to be understood as that which constitute hours, minutes and seconds. Time will be looked at as a particular season within one's life. Similar emphasis will be placed on the word Weightiness and the important part it plays in one's season.

As Warriors of Time we need to know how to, and when to begin to prepare ourselves for our Season, which will be in our time. However, when it happens we will not be able to select the category we would wish our season to embrace for it can appear in all of the categories aforementioned.

However before we talk about weightiness in the context of it manifesting itself through any of the following, psychological, sociological, biological, philosophical and spiritual, let us understand how time or season can be described.

Time/season can be interpreted as being a period representing, what one may best describe as ponderousness; heaviness; impressive; having the power to convince; and a place of prominence. All of these speaks to a time of heavy weights.

Yes, Seasons bring with it a degree of weightiness, and requires a certain lifestyle. The real reason for Time/season being weighty is to steady us during that period, when power, privileges, and opportunities are present. It serves the same purpose an anchor does to a ship. It does not matter how large or small a sea vessel may be, it's anchor is designed to compliment its needs.

It is very interesting how so many Christians long for their season to come, but not having any understanding that with it comes weights, comparable to that particular season. If there is no weight, that particular season will be very short lived. Weights is inclusive of such things as order, humility and patience.

My brothers and sisters, I am sure you can attest to seeing how many person's season seemed to last far longer than others, causing you to conclude that perhaps they are more blessed than others.

You would even question how God's favor is not fair. In fact, we have heard many preachers allude to that statement as being a fact.

Whereas it may be true, I believe it is all due to the weightiness attached to one's season and their ability to endure in such circumstances, demanding order, patience and humility.

Here is something else for us to ponder as it relates to our understanding of the word weightiness.

Let's look at the weightiness of God's Holiness. Holiness is weighty. Perhaps that is why so many Christians find it very hard to live in God's season of Holiness for their lives.

Holiness is weighty, and a Christian must view weights as fulfilling a specific need. So then, what are some of these weights what will steady us in perilous times, permitting us to remain holy?

Well, it cannot be anything like light and fluffy preaching; not sentimentality or self-help, coupled with a you can do it theology; not words on how you can become rich and healthy. What will steady us during tempestuous times, while living holy, will be deep thoughts, weighty thoughts and heavy doctrines.

I return to the subject of understanding the many mental forms through which weightiness operates during one's season, and how Christians are expected to deal with them, as they will be confronted by them in many ways:

Psychological Weightiness

Let us briefly look at Psychological weightiness and the very important part order, humility or patience plays.

In the lives of Christians, psychological weights can be seen as having to deal with a concern, which ultimately brings about pressure on the mind, causing one to be constantly challenged to find a way to correct it. Mental weightiness to a Christian may address such concerns as having to make decisions at the right time, regards taking risk, without being viewed as possessing those traits inherent in one who gambles. Theirs must be as one exhibiting great faith in God.

Sociological Weightiness

Let's now consider Sociological weightiness as it relates to order, humility and patience. In the lives of Christians, sociological weightiness can be viewed as having to deal with the ever increasing social problems within the society and the failure of man to cooperate for the eradication of it and the growth and development of a better world. They constantly live with a burning desire to find the correct approach to help eradicate sin, for in it lies the real answer to our problems.

The weightiness in this category, through which a Christian Sociologist bears, is that they constantly wonder, if they are doing their best in this period that is filled with violence, to stop this ever increasing state being experienced by society.

Biological Weightiness

Biological weightiness as it relates to order, humility and patience, in the life of a Christian biologist, can be viewed as not being able to find a way to curb the flow of communicable diseases, resulting in the death of many innocent young individuals; but still possessing this burning desire to not quit until a major discovery is found. If it is their season, remarkable discoveries will eventually be made, and the extent to which these will happen will be based on them recognizing the need for order, humility and patience.

Philosophical Weightiness

Philosophical weightiness as it relates to order, humility and patience, may be viewed through the expressed understanding of a philosopher being able to articulate and agree on a point that could improve mankind's ability to enjoy universal peace and economic freedom; but still possessing the desire to pursue it until it is realized.

The philosophical difference which seem to separate many is the view that God should have never permitted sin into His creation, by so doing we have developed into a society lacking the ability to cooperate. If the purpose for original sin is understood, man's understanding of it would truly give us an appreciation how a Wise and Holy God operates.

Spiritual Weightiness

Spiritual weightiness as it relates to order, patience and humility, is that which is experienced in the lives of Christians, when they find themselves constantly battling, not being able to achieve their desires to fully attain a good relationship with both God and man. There constantly exists within them a fight and they are determined not to give in until the power over evil prevails.

CHAPTER EIGHT

When The Wait Is Over

Most blessings are preceded by time, which is a waiting session, that usually ends in a period of celebration. However time also lends itself to moments of reflection that will include some regrettable discourses. This is when the time of waiting, becomes a burden and is therefore not seen as an introduction to some great blessings.

I repeat, It would appear then, that a blessing is very often preceded by a burden.

So what are burdens? Burdens are usually the devil's tool to get us away from where we should be in order to prevent us from being in the right position to receive our blessings.

Burdens differ based on the blessings that have been approved by God for the individual. Some are weightier than others, due to the blessing that is in store for the burden bearers.

Most burdens come at us in the form of having to wait for ones blessing.

I believe that it is safe to conclude that very often, waiting can be very expensive and nerve wrecking, thus a heavy burden. As a result, many persons succumb to its pressure. Until we understand that there are many things in life which requires us having to wait, we will always fail in this test from the devil.

Here is a good example.

A lady who was with child for nine months, looks back at those periods when child bearing was very uncomfortable: How her movements were limited, how the things she ate were very restricted, how the clothes she wore were special, during those nine months.

Because she understands that a period of nine months must be accomplished, she bears the discomforts accompanying the birth of her child.

What was even more terrible, was when the time came for the delivery. This is when the most excruciating moments prevailed. These were the times when mothering was at its worst. These were the times when the person along with God, had to deal with what is known as labor pains.

When it was all over, she is presented with a baby, a new life to claim as her child.

The mother then looks back at those times of misery and how she vowed that she would not have another baby. But when that period is over, she looks back and say that it was really worth it all. It was worth the wait.

Here is another example.

As a former Principal of High Schools, I have witnessed the joy being experienced by graduates as they walk across the stage to receive their diploma. To all of them it took twelve long years to arrive at that period in time, knowing quite well that there were no short cuts to their destination.

Many were the expressions from valedictorians as they spoke on behalf of their classmates. They would try to relive the many trying moments during their junior and senior years of school life. They would reflect on the difficult times many teachers took them through, and how they were tempted to give up.

They would mention such things as detention, suspensions and principal visits, as being a part of their twelve months sojourn.

But the thanks they expressed to both teachers and parents, would always accompany their closing remarks. There is nothing like the joy one experiences, when the wait is over.

The first lesson I wish to leave with you is vividly shown are the two examples given.

When a waiting period is over, whose who had to wait is taken to another level, a new dimension. Yes, many times they were tempted to feel depressed, and they wanted to give up.

But that which was experienced prior, no longer prevails. You are at a new level. It is expected that we be prepared to embrace a new time, or a new season.

Every level is preceded by a time of waiting. Again how we handle it, would determine whether we are ready for another level.

I repeat, it does not matter how long the wait, how difficult the wait may be, or the purpose for which we wait. The purpose for which one waits is very important to them. That is what really matters.

If it is just waiting for the bus to arrive, if it is waiting for lunch to be completed, if it is for a word from The Lord; to those individuals, they all carry the same degree of importance. They will be advanced to that next level.

Another thing which comes along when the waiting is over, is being able to testify about what you have been through.

It's very difficult to give an encouraging word to someone about what it will be like, unless you are able to talk about what it is like being out on the other side. Far too many times we try to testify about how good God has been to us, without persons being able to recall what you were like yesterday. Don't talk about a wonderful change in your life, until the change is evidenced. When the wait is over, the change will be visible.

Here is something else which accompanies the end to wait. When your waiting is over, God receives all the glory.

If you are sure you have received that which you have prayed for, then you do not talk about how you came out by doing what you did. All you will find joy in is talking about how God lifted you out of your miry clay and planted you on a rock to stay. Yes when the wait is over, you give God all the praise, and all the glory.

Brethren, when you are successfully over your waiting period, many will be blessed as a result of seeing what God can do, and has done through you. That is why being able to share a real testimony with others is so very important for others to have their faith in God strengthened

There are three outstanding incidents recorded in the Bible which support how very powerful the results from waiting are, when it is all over.

The raising of Lazarus.

We are told that Jesus was contacted at least four days before the death of His dear friend Lazarus. He was told that he whom he loved very much, was sick. But before beginning to travel to his friend's home, he stayed there for another four days.

The scripture leaves us to understand that there could have been three reasons for this delay.

One reason could be that God would receive Glory out of this event.

The second reason could be that the act would be a lasting testimony to those who witnessed it, and to those with whom this incident will be shared.

The third reason could be

Not only does the story of Lazarus reveal how powerful an impact one experiences when the waiting period is over, but the woman with an issue of blood, comes forward to testify that she is healed.

In the Gospel recorded by St Matthew 9:20, we are told that she was sick for twelve years, and had tried many doctors in search of being made well, but she was not successful until she touched the edge of Jesus' garment. Immediately she was made healthy. In other words, the end of her waiting period had come. She moved on to another level of wholeness, and life was no longer the same.

I don't believe we can put a number to the many times she had to testify about how Jesus healed her. In addition, every time she talked about it, God was glorified.

When the waiting season is over, you can't help but share your experiences with all and sundry. You can't help but give thanks and glory to God, for where He brought you from.

As we continue, let's look at Blind Bartaemus who sat for many years by the gate asking for help.

I do believe there may have been times, due to weather conditions among many other incidents, when he begged in vain.

The Gospel recorded by St Mark 10:46-52, speaks to a particular visit Jesus made to the city of Jericho, but His encounter with Bartimaeus did not take place until He was on His way leaving the city. He began to cry out to Jesus for help. We are told that his cry made Jesus stand still and command that he be brought to Him. The results of this encounter, left Bartimaeus being able to see.

Again can we imagine the many times he had to share his testimony with so many? Can we imagine the many persons who were present at this miracle, and how it impacted their understanding of God?

It all happened to blind Bartimaeus, when his waiting period was over.

Brethren, there are countless others in this 21st Century who could speak to what happened to them, when their waiting period was over. They found themselves blessed beyond measure. They are able to testify about experiencing what can only be described as a supernatural act, which only God can perform.

As I close this chapter, I want to visit an event recorded in the Book of Revelation, as it relates specifically to the subject of, and an incident where, persons were concerned about when their waiting period would be over.

John the writer of the Book of Revelation writes about a peculiar scene that's taking place under the altar in Chapter 6:7-11. This sight takes place at the opening of the fifth seal, when a specific question is being asked by some souls hidden under the altar. The, question was, 'how long O Lord.'

As one reads on, we see where the answer is given in this seal. The answer is, "until all...."

In as much as there are differing views regarding who those souls were, I believe that they represented the church, past present and future. This is because it seems as if, this question seemed to be the cry of a weary church.

My brothers and sisters, The church has been following her Lord, from Bethlehem to Calvary looking forward to, with great anticipation for His return. They have experienced persecutions upon persecutions, expecting the immediate return of their Lord. However the glowing dream of a quick conquest over all evil passes away, and the picture of a weary, persecuted church, takes its place and the voice of its anguish is daily heard. "How long, O Lord, how long."

John writes very descriptively, as he sees the souls of these martyrs, as being under the altar, which is situated at the foot of the altar in heaven. This altar is at the feet of Christ.

Their constant cry is as one longing to be revenged.

Yes they have been terribly persecuted, and their bodies totally destroyed. Yes, their souls are safe under the altar. But although they were safe, their cry was still as one wanting to know how long. It appears to be a cry for revenge, which only God can perform.

The cause for which they suffered and died, was for the Gospel. They committed themselves to Him. And It is without a doubt that they believed that He will seek vengeance on their behalf. There only pressing concern was, when.

Then comes the answer, "until all of the saints have been sealed." This is when it will all happen. This will be when the final wait is over.

CONCLUSION

When Waiting is not Debatable

There are some mundane things and events around which all of us human beings function. These events have become so much a part of us, that we dare not pretend that they do not play integral roles. Therefore, we find it very hard to survive without them.

I speak of such events pertaining to cultural celebrations, religious festivals, and social events. No one dares to, remove them or ignore the importance these periods play in the annual calendar of celebration without having to find oneself involved in very harsh debates.

Don't tell me that I should not celebrate my birthday, Christmas, New Years, Independence Day, Thanksgiving Day, Junkanoo Festival and the list goes on. These periods are not debatable.

It matters very little what name a people would give to their cultural celebrations, or their religious festivals, they believe that these should be celebrated.

The important thing is that they pay high tribute to these seasonal activities, and look forward with great anticipation to acknowledging these occasions. Many times they wait impatiently for them to arrive, void of having the power to hurry their arrival. They can do nothing but to wait on time. This is when waiting is not debatable.

So I wish to reiterate the fact that there are many things which we have no control of concerning their arrival. Christmas will come on the 25th of December, in each year, without fail, should the world be in existence. Battles, wars, famine, catastrophic conditions will not altar it's arrival.

So it is with the many other events.

A child will be born at the completion of the pregnancy period, regardless of any of the above. Persons will die whenever the time appointed, regardless of their infirmity, regardless of any of the above.

The truth of the matter is that there are some things for which waiting is not debatable. Certain things are not within our power to perform.

So it is with many things that are spiritual. God has the last say. He is the ultimate. There is no one else who can cause things to happen, without an ulterior motive. When He acts, it is always in the fullness of time, kurios. It is usually when the desire to question the presence, power, and purpose of God, is paramount.

Brethren this is when I ask that we not debate our waiting period. It is usually that period of time when the devil is at his best to frustrate the plan of God for us.

Don't argue, just wait on Him as a waiter does on a customer. Busy yourself while waiting with great expectancy. God will come through for you.